Bus to
A Techie's Coincidental Journey With A Spiritual Master

By
Atul Jadhav

First Edition: May 2025
Copyright © 2025 by Atul Jadhav
All rights reserved.

Preface

As a boy in Satara, Maharashtra, I chased the divine in the Kshetra Mahuli temple's chants, their echoes weaving through incense and the eternal hills, but the truths I sought slipped away like monsoon mist. At 25, I was a software engineer in Pune, coding in Kharadi's glass towers, my nights spent wrestling with life's mysteries—Why am I here? What lies beyond the visible? On Monday, June 7, 2021, as India emerged from COVID-19's grip, restrictions lifted, and cautious hope returned, I boarded a bus from Satara to Pune. A stranger sat beside me, his serene calm silencing the world's clamor. In two and a half hours, his words unraveled existence, revealing Brahma—the infinite consciousness binding all. His fleeting touch sparked a golden light, a glimpse of eternity that shattered my doubts and set me on a path to bliss.

Now, in May 2025, I write from New York, where I've lived since December 2022, working in IT amid skyscrapers and restless dreams. The stranger's wisdom anchors me, his detachment a beacon across continents. I return to India yearly, each encounter deepening my practice, his presence one with the infinite. In 2023, I urged him to share his truth, facilitating a book's publication, translated into German, Spanish, and French to reach global seekers. I'm no guru—just a coder from Satara who stumbled upon eternity on a bus. Through this book and my free workshops, I pass on the light, inviting you to find your path. Maharashtra's rivers, flowing from the Western Ghats, mirror the journey—eternal, ever-moving, yet always home. The infinite is closer than you know, waiting within. Step forward, heart open, and uncover the truth that's always been yours.

TABLE OF CONTENTS

1: A BOY FROM SATARA 7
2: THE MONDAY BUS 11
3: THE QUIET STRANGER 13
4: A SPARK OF CURIOSITY 15
5: WHAT LIES BEYOND? 17
6: THE DREAM OF THE WORLD 19
7: WHY ARE WE HERE? 21
8: CHASING SHADOWS 23
9: ECHOES OF THE PAST 25
10: THE LIGHT OF ENLIGHTENMENT 27
11: QUESTIONING EVERYTHING 29
12: THE ESSENCE OF BRAHMA 31
13: THE DANCE OF EXISTENCE 33
14: THE HIDDEN SELF 35
15: DECODING THE MIND 37
16: GUIDES OR ILLUSIONS? 39
17: WORDS WITHOUT WINGS 41
18: THE ENDLESS WHY 43
19: BREAKING FREE FROM FAITH 45
20: EMPTY RITUALS 47
21: TIME FOR TRUTH 49
22: LIFTING THE FOG 51
23: THE WEIGHT OF DESIRE 53

24: THE MIRROR OF AWARENESS 55
25: THE ILLUSION OF CONTROL 57
26: THE ROOTS OF SUFFERING 59
27: THE JOY WITHIN 61
28: BEYOND GOOD AND EVIL 63
29: THE ETERNAL NOW 65
30: THE INFINITE WITHIN 67
31: THE PLAY OF FORMS 69
32: THE SILENCE OF TRUTH 71
33: THE FIRE OF INQUIRY 73
34: THE UNITY OF ALL 75
35: THE VEIL OF WORDS 77
36: THE WEIGHT OF DOUBT 79
37: THE DANCE OF DETACHMENT 81
38: THE LIGHT OF COMPASSION 83
39: THE END OF SEEKING 85
40: THE TOUCH OF ETERNITY 87
41: A JOURNEY UNFINISHED 89

1: A Boy from Satara

Satara's hills cradled my childhood, their emerald slopes rolling under a sky so vast it seemed to hold the secrets of the universe. Born in 1995 near the Kshetra Mahuli temple, I grew up in a modest home where the scent of wet earth mingled with the fragrance of marigolds offered to stone deities. The Krishna River, winding through Satara, glistened like a silver thread, its waters carrying tales of ancient pilgrims and Maratha warriors. My father, a schoolteacher, filled our evenings with stories of Shivaji Maharaj, his voice rich as the Venna River, recounting battles atop Pratapgad Fort, where the Maratha king's courage shaped Maharashtra's soul. My mother, her hands deftly shaping puran poli, hummed Krishna's songs, her love weaving a warmth that rivaled the temple's oil lamps flickering at dusk.

As a boy, I'd wander to the temple, its sandstone walls etched with centuries of devotion, mimicking sadhus in their saffron robes. Their chants, rhythmic as the monsoon's pulse, stirred questions: Why pour milk over stone idols? Was God in the lamps, the starry sky, or the hills that stood sentinel over Satara? Those mysteries lingered, a quiet ache, even as I ran through mango orchards, their branches heavy with fruit, the air sweet with promise. Satara, nestled in the Western Ghats, was a land of contrasts—lush valleys fed by monsoon rains, rugged forts like Ajinkyatara standing proud, their stones whispering of a Maratha empire that defied Mughal might. The region's history, from Shivaji's guerrilla tactics to the ancient Buddhist caves at Karad, rooted me in a past that felt alive, urging me to seek beyond the visible. In college, I studied computer science in Pune, but Satara's call never faded. I devoured spiritual texts—the Gita, Upanishads, Kabir's verses—searching for answers in their ancient wisdom. I joined a meditation circle, sitting cross-legged under Satara's banyan trees, the dawn air sharp, hoping to touch the divine. Yoga in the orchards, my breath syncing with the rustle of leaves, brought fleeting peace, but truth slipped away, a mist over the Krishna River. At 25, I was a software engineer in Pune's Kharadi district, coding in a glass-walled office, my nights spent in a cramped flat, the city's neon hum drowning my thoughts. Weekends, I rode the Shivashahi bus to Satara, sinking into my mother's dal and rice, debating karma and fate with my father, his logic sharp, my questions sharper. Rituals—mantras, fasts, temple visits—offered comfort but no clarity, like a half-remembered song.

Pune, sprawling across the Deccan Plateau, was a city of contrasts—tech hubs rising beside ancient wadas, the Mula-Mutha River choked with urban dreams, yet carrying echoes of Peshwa rule. Its history, from the Maratha capital under Bajirao to the British cantonment, pulsed in its streets, a reminder of time's relentless march. My Pune life—deadlines, meetings, promotions—felt hollow, a chase for something unnamed. I'd scroll spiritual blogs, attempt meditation, only to be pulled back by notifications, the city's rhythm unyielding. Satara's orchards remained my refuge, their shade cooling my restless heart, whispering of a divine voice I'd sensed as a child, hidden in the hills 'eternal embrace.

In June 2021, India exhaled as COVID-19 restrictions lifted, the pandemic's shadow lingering in cautious crowds and masked faces. Buses resumed, a lifeline restored, and I booked a ticket for the 9:00 AM Shivashahi from Satara to Pune, seat 21, a two-and-a-half-hour journey to my Kharadi cubicle. The Western Ghats, their peaks shrouded in pre-monsoon mist, framed the highway, their ancient basalt carved by eons, a testament to nature's quiet power. Maharashtra's spiritual legacy—Pandharpur's Vithoba, Kolhapur's Mahalakshmi—infused the land, urging me to seek the infinite. Little did I know, that Monday ride on June 7 would ignite a spark, transforming my quest into a flame, guided by a stranger whose wisdom would echo Satara's hills, leading me to the truth I'd always sought.

2: The Monday Bus

June 7, 2021, broke with a humid glow, the air thick with the promise of monsoon rains and cautious hope post-COVID-19. At 8:45 AM, I reached the bus stand, backpack heavy with books and snacks, mask snug, the crowd a mix of relief and wariness—chai vendors steaming kettles, travelers clutching tickets, a scene alive with energy. My ticket for the 9:00 AM Shivashahi to Pune, seat 21, promised a journey back to the urban pulse.

The red-and-silver bus gleamed, a symbol of normalcy restored. I boarded, navigating masked passengers, newspapers rustling, the air tinged with optimism. Seat 22 held a stranger in a white kurta, mask below his chin, eyes fixed on the horizon, radiating a stillness that silenced the bustle. No phone, no book, just a calm vast as a river's flow, eternal yet grounded. I mumbled a greeting, voice muffled, and slid into the window seat, glass cool, the bus lurching forward, pulling us onto the highway, sugarcane fields swaying outside.

The stranger's presence was a quiet force, his detachment a contrast to my restless thoughts—Pune's deadlines, my flat's clutter, the weekend's warmth fading. I glanced at him, hands folded, face serene. My bag rested on my lap, notebook inside, a habit for capturing thoughts—code, musings, questions. Today, an urge to write stirred, sensing something momentous, though unnamed. Pune loomed—team demands, urban sprawl—but the stranger's calm hinted at a journey beyond, toward the infinite I'd chased since childhood.

3: The Quiet Stranger

The Shivashahi bus rolled through sugarcane fields under a sky heavy with monsoon clouds. The stranger beside me sat still, hands folded, white kurta pristine, his calm a quiet force that hushed the chatter of masked passengers, their faces reflecting post-COVID relief. No phone, no book, just a presence vast as a river, mirroring the eternal.

I shifted in my window seat, glass warm, my thoughts restless—Pune's deadlines, my failed meditations, the elusive peace I'd sought since childhood. The stranger's silence pressed on me, heavy yet inviting, a challenge to my chaos. I fidgeted, adjusting my bag, its weight like my doubts. I cleared my throat, mask muffling my voice. "Hot day, isn't it?" I said, the air thick with June's humidity. He turned, eyes warm yet piercing, seeing past my words. "Heat's just a thought," he said, voice soft but resonant, cutting through my restless mind. The words landed oddly, simple yet profound, hinting at a truth beyond weather. His detachment mirrored my inner noise—stress, quests for answers—yet his calm suggested a path through it.

"You from around here?" I ventured, voice soft through my mask. His smile was faint, calm infinite. "I'm from everywhere," he said, voice warm, detached, a riddle echoing the sadhus who spoke of the divine in all things. The words stirred curiosity. I opened my notebook, pen in hand, sensing this was no chance meeting, a moment to shift my path toward the infinite.

4: A Spark of Curiosity

The stranger's words—"Heat's just a thought"—lingered, stirring a spark of curiosity in my chest, a mix of awe and unease. The Shivashahi bus wound through sugarcane fields, the landscape framed by the Western Ghats' peaks, shrouded in mist. I shifted in my window seat, notebook open, pen poised, the stranger's calm a quiet force beside me, his white kurta catching sunlight.

"I work in Pune, software stuff," I said, testing the waters, voice muffled by my mask. The stranger nodded, a faint smile on his lips, his calm vast. "Pune's got heart," he said, voice soft, hinting at depths I couldn't grasp. I spilled details—my coding job in Kharadi, my love for the hills. Hesitantly, I ventured deeper, the stranger's calm pulling me. "I've been chasing something bigger," I confessed, voice low. "Enlightenment, maybe. Yoga, books, meditation—I'm stuck, running in circles." The admission felt raw.

His gaze softened, eyes piercing yet warm, seeing my soul through the mask. "What's enlightenment to you?" he asked, voice gentle but sharp, peeling back my vague hopes. The question struck, stripping my dreams—freedom from stress, lasting happiness. "I don't know," I admitted, pen pausing, heart racing. "Maybe peace? Not worrying, not chasing?" His smile deepened, serene, as if my struggle was a cloud he saw through. "Let's dig deeper," he said, voice a quiet invitation to the unknown. "What's the source of all this—life, the world, you?" My pulse quickened, the question ringing, high in the mountains, where pilgrims sought grace.

15

"Science says energy, maybe?" I offered, coder's mind grasping fragments, picturing quantum fields from textbooks. "But I don't know what's behind it." The stranger's calm urged me beyond, to question the questions, his presence a mirror to the timeless spirit I sought. "You've been seeking," he said, as if reading my thoughts, his voice warm, detached. "That's the start. Keep asking." I scribbled, sensing a fire sparking, pulling me toward a truth I'd always chased, guided by a mysterious stranger whose wisdom seemed to flow from the infinite.

5: What Lies Beyond?

The stranger's question—"What's the source of all this?"—echoed, a challenge I couldn't sidestep. The Shivashahi bus wound through the Western Ghats, sugarcane fields stretching under a sky heavy with monsoon clouds. I fumbled, coder's brain grasping at college physics—quantum fields, cosmic origins—my voice uncertain through my mask. "Maybe energy?" I offered, feeling foolish, picturing particles dancing in a void. "Quantum stuff, fields?" I glanced at my notebook, pen trembling, its pages crowded with the stranger's insights.

He nodded, calm unshaken, white kurta catching sunlight, his presence rooted in the eternal. "Science sees fields—vibrations, particles, energy dancing," he said, voice steady. "But why do they exist? What's behind the dance?" The question rang, resonant, calling to a mystery no algorithm could solve.

I stared, mind blank. "It's Brahma," he said, voice clear, alive, a truth that stirred the air like monsoon winds. "The eternal consciousness, not nothing, not something, but all—infinite, alive, joyful. Enlightenment is knowing you're one with it, no separation." The words struck like lightning, setting my heart ablaze.

"So, I'm Brahma?" I asked, half-laughing, half-awed, voice muffled, the idea vast. His gaze held, rooted in truth, calm boundless. "Yes," he said, smiling, "but you're lost in a dream of being separate, a story spun by the mind." The words landed, heavy as monsoon rains.

"But it feels so real," I said, tapping the seat, its fabric rough, grounding me in the ordinary. "My job, my family—how's that a dream?" His calm enveloped me, voice gentle but firm. "They're real as a dream—vivid, fleeting. Brahma's the dreamer, the dream, the truth." The metaphor painted the universe as a play, intimate yet infinite. I scribbled, hand shaking, heart pounding, as if I'd stumbled on a secret.

"How do I wake up?" I asked, voice soft, pen racing. "Start by seeing," he said, calm infinite, his words a map to a forgotten home. "See the fields, your work, your fears, as Brahma's play. Then look deeper—what sees them?" His presence urged me inward, to a truth he seemed to live, his wisdom flowing boundless.

6: The Dream of the World

The stranger's declaration—that I was Brahma, lost in a dream—stirred a question as vast as the Western Ghats' peaks. The Shivashahi bus wound through sugarcane fields, the landscape a hymn to the fertile earth. "If Brahma's everything," I asked, voice tentative, notebook open, pen poised, "where did the world come from?" The question felt like a stone tossed into a river, ripples spreading toward an unseen shore.

The stranger turned, his white kurta catching sunlight, his calm serene. "No one truly knows," he said, voice soft, clear. "Not sages with their hymns, nor scientists with telescopes peering at stars. Some speak of a cosmic cycle—expansion, collapse, rebirth—but it's Brahma's play, a fleeting illusion, like a monsoon mist rising, vivid yet gone by noon." The words rippled through me, chilling yet freeing.

I scribbled, heart racing. "So, no creator?" I pressed, pen hovering, seeking logic. The stranger shook his head, his calm vast, as if the question dissolved in his presence. "Brahma doesn't craft—it flows, becomes," he said, his voice a gentle tide. "The world's a shadow your mind casts, not the truth, like a dream you wake from at dawn, leaving only Brahma's light."

I pictured Pune, now a tech hub, its river choked with urban dreams. Was that a dream too? "So, nothing's real?" I asked, voice tinged with disbelief, glancing at the passengers, their lives a tapestry—farmers, students, devotees, each a story. "Only Brahma," he said, smile faint but warm. "The rest is a story your mind spins, a dream you mistake for home."

I leaned back, notebook filling, the idea unsettling yet liberating. "But it feels solid," I said, touching the seat's fabric, grounding myself in the ordinary, my coder's life—deadlines, emails—feeling real. "The fields, my family—how's it an illusion?" His gaze drifted to the horizon, calm a quiet force. "Feel the fields, live your life—but know they're waves on Brahma's ocean. They rise, fall, but the ocean remains."

"How do I see past the dream?" I asked, voice quieter, notebook a map of new terrain. "Start by questioning," he said, his calm infinite. "Not just the world, but the 'you' who sees it. Find what's real." The stranger's presence, serene, made the world light, a play of shadows on Brahma's canvas.

7: Why Are We Here?

The idea of the world as Brahma's dream sparked a frustration as sharp as the Western Ghats' cliffs. The Shivashahi bus traced the highway, sugarcane fields rolling toward the horizon. The stranger's calm, a quiet force beside me, his white kurta catching sunlight, urged me to voice the ache in my chest. "If it's all a dream," I said, leaning forward, voice tight, "what's the point of living?" My notebook lay open, pen poised, the question heavy. His eyes softened, calm radiating vastness. "Life pushes to survive, create, adapt," he said, voice steady. "But its deepest call is to feel the joy of being, the bliss that's your essence, Brahma's pulse in every heart." The words turned a rusty lock in my mind, stirring a memory of wordless happiness lost in Pune's relentless pace.

I frowned, picturing my Kharadi cubicle—buggy code, meetings, rent—stress drowning any joy. "Joy?" I said, almost scoffing, my coder's life a far cry from bliss. "I'm buried in deadlines, expectations." His smile was gentle, calm a clear sky over my clouds. "Joy lives within, not in things," he said, his voice a gentle tide. "Life's highs and lows—success, failure, love, loss—hide it. Enlightenment peels back the veil, reveals bliss that never fades."

I scribbled, heart quickening, the idea as vast as the landscape. "So, it's always there?" I asked, pen racing. "Always," he said, voice warm, detached. "Why hide it?" I asked, voice softer, picturing my Pune nights, chasing peace through meditation, only to falter. "The mind builds walls—names, roles, wants," he said. "You think you're a coder, a son, a dreamer. Those are stories, not you. Brahma's joy is your core, but you chase shadows."

The words stung, exposing my frantic pace—Pune's traffic, my team's demands, the fleeting thrill of a solved bug, then the next task. "How do I find it?" I asked, voice low. "Start where you are," he said, calm infinite, his words a map to a forgotten home. "Watch your life, your thoughts, without clinging. Joy's there, waiting."

"Like meditation?" I asked, picturing my Pune attempts, distracted by urban hum. "Meditation helps," he said, "but it's seeing. See Brahma in noise, silence, you, flowing through every moment." The stranger's presence made joy tangible, a pulse I could touch if I let go.

8: Chasing Shadows

The Shivashahi bus traced the highway, sugarcane fields stretching toward the horizon. The stranger's calm, a quiet force beside me, his white kurta catching sunlight, urged me to voice my unease. "Buildings, empires—they collapse," I said, voice heavy, notebook open, pen poised. "Why bother if it all fades?" The question felt like a gust scattering dreams.

The stranger nodded, gaze detached, his calm vast. "Nothing endures," he said, voice soft, clear. "Cities, fame, humanity's mark—a cosmic flare, an asteroid—Pune's towers would be dust." The words rippled through me, chilling yet freeing. I scribbled, heart racing. "So, it's pointless?" I asked, voice uneasy, my coder's life—deadlines, promotions, my parents' pride—feeling fleeting. His calm held my protest gently. "Material things vanish," he said, smile kind. "Houses, empires, names—they're shadows. Brahma remains, eternal, the truth you seek."

The word "shadows" struck, a blade through my chase for meaning. I leaned back, notebook filling. "But we build—careers, families—for a reason," I said, defending my world. "They matter," he said, detachment warm. "Like waves to the ocean—real for a moment, gone. Live them, don't cling. Brahma's your home, not the shadows you chase."

"How do I seek Brahma?" I asked, voice quieter, notebook a map of new terrain. "Start by seeing," he said. "See your work, your dreams, as passing. What remains?" I thought of my goals—better job, bigger flat, a life of meaning. "It's hard to let go," I admitted. "You don't let go," he said, his voice a gentle tide. "See through. Live fully, know it's a play. Brahma's the stage, actor, audience, eternal in every moment."

9: Echoes of the Past

The stranger's words—that Brahma was eternal, beyond time's echoes—ignited a hunger. The Shivashahi bus rolled on, sugarcane fields stretching under a sky heavy with clouds. "So, we're like dinosaurs?" I asked, voice wavering, notebook open, pen poised. "Here today, gone, forgotten?" The question felt heavy.

The stranger's smile was faint, his calm glowing. "Dinosaurs ruled millions of years," he said, voice soft, piercing. "Billions of lives, their triumphs—illusions, dust now. So are your achievements, fleeting echoes in Brahma's silence." The words stirred awe and resistance, chilling yet freeing.

I scribbled, heart racing. "That's grim," I said, pen hesitating, picturing my career—leading projects, climbing the tech ladder, my parents' pride in my degree. His calm held my protest. "It's freedom," he said. "Brahma was before dinosaurs, is now, forever. Find that, and the past's echoes fade."

I leaned back, notebook filling, the idea settling. Freedom felt distant, yet his truth made history weightless, a ripple in Brahma's sea. "Let go of achievements?" I asked, voice low, pen trembling. "Find what never fades," he said, gaze steady, seeing through time. "Achievements give meaning," I said. "They drive, but where?" he said, detachment kind. "Meaning's in Brahma, not the chase. Live goals, know they pass."

"How do I find what doesn't fade?" I asked, voice softer, notebook a map of new terrain. "Look within," he said, his voice a gentle tide. "See the 'you' that's not a coder, not a son. That's Brahma, eternal in every moment."

10: The Light of Enlightenment

The stranger's words—that Brahma was eternal—ignited a hunger as fierce as monsoon winds. The Shivashahi bus traced the highway, sugarcane fields stretching under a sky heavy with clouds. "What's enlightenment, really?" I asked, voice tight with longing, notebook open, pen poised. His gaze softened, eyes piercing yet warm, seeing past my roles to a truth as vast as the sky. "It's seeing you're Brahma," he said, voice steady, a lighthouse in a storm. "No 'you' apart, no separation. The dream of being separate dissolves, revealing the infinite light within, joyful, whole." The words struck like a spark, setting my heart ablaze.

"But I'm sitting here," I said, voice defiant, confused, gripping the seat's fabric, grounding myself in the ordinary. "A role Brahma plays," he said. "Enlightenment drops the mask, reveals the whole." He outlined steps, clear, unadorned: "Learn truth from those who know, reflect deeply, focus your mind, merge with Brahma. No chants, no temples—just seeing, clear as the dawn."

I scribbled, pen racing, heart pounding. "That simple?" I asked, breathless, voice low, picturing my Pune meditations, distracted by urban hum. "Simple, not easy," he said, smile faint, warm. "The mind loves masks—your job, fears, plans. Seeing through takes effort, but it's yours, eternal yet reachable."

"How do I know I'm on the path?" I asked, voice softer, notebook filling. His gaze held mine, serene, infinite. "You'll feel it—quiet joy, lightness, a peace that stays. The world remains, no longer your cage." I wrote, memories flooding—moments when life felt effortless, coding a perfect algorithm in Pune, laughing with my parents. Glimpses of enlightenment? "Does everyone find it?" I asked, thinking of my family. "Everyone can," he said, his voice a gentle tide, "but few look. The world's loud, like Pune's streets, drowning the silence."

"What if I fail?" I asked, voice small, fear creeping. "You can't fail," he said, calm a gentle force. "Brahma's you, just remembering, flowing to its source." I scribbled, notebook a map, each word a step toward the light he spoke of, a truth vast yet intimate, a home I'd never left.

11: Questioning Everything

The stranger's promise of enlightenment sparked an eagerness. The Shivashahi bus rolled on, sugarcane fields under a sky heavy with clouds. "How do I start finding Brahma, enlightenment?" I asked, leaning forward, notebook open, pen poised. His gaze pierced, serene, eyes warm yet infinite, making my questions feel urgent yet small. "Question everything," he said, voice clear, unhurried. "Your beliefs, your books, your science—test them. Seek truth yourself, not what others give." The words framed doubt as sacred, a tool to peel layers to the infinite.

I hesitated, picturing my parents' puja room, incense curling, rituals since childhood. "Even traditions?" I asked, voice wavering, doubt stirring unease. He nodded, detachment serene. "Yes," he said, smile warm, his voice a gentle tide. "Borrowed faith blinds. Truth demands your eyes, clear as the dawn."

I scribbled, hand shaking. "They feel true," I said, voice soft, picturing my father's karma talks. "They're part of me." His smile was kind, calm a gentle anchor. "They're part of your story, not Brahma," he said. "Test them, keep what holds, let go what doesn't."

"What if I'm lost without them?" I asked, fear creeping, pen pausing. "Truth finds an open heart," he said, his voice a gentle tide. "Be honest, admit errors. Brahma's waiting, flowing to its source." I wrote, memories flooding—college debates in Pune, questioning God, retreating to rituals for comfort. I pictured Pune's tech hub, coding, meetings, approval's race—another blind faith. "How do I

29

question without losing myself?" I asked, voice steadier, notebook filling. "You don't lose," he said. "You find. The 'self' you fear losing is a mask. Brahma's your core, eternal in every moment."

"Start small," he said, as if reading my thoughts, his voice a gentle tide. "One belief, one doubt." His serene presence made every word a guidepost, urging me into the unknown with courage.

12: The Essence of Brahma

The stranger's call to question everything stirred a mystery. The Shivashahi bus rolled on, sugarcane fields under a sky heavy with clouds. "What's Brahma, really?" I asked, voice soft, notebook open, pen trembling, the question a whisper from my childhood.

His gaze was serene, his calm infinite. "Brahma's the source, the essence," he said, voice clear. "Not a thing, not a void—the infinite consciousness, alive, joyful, whole, appearing as all, like the sky holding clouds, stars, storms, yet untouched." The words painted Brahma as the root of existence.

I scribbled, heart pounding. "Not a creator?" I asked, pen racing, picturing my mother's prayers, her faith in a divine maker. "No," he said, smile warm, his voice a gentle tide. "Brahma doesn't create—it is. The world, you, all forms are Brahma's play, like waves on an ocean, rising, falling, but always the ocean."

"How do I know Brahma?" I asked, voice eager. "Look within," he said, detachment infinite. "See what's aware—beyond thoughts, roles, fears. That's Brahma, like the dawn, clear and eternal." I leaned back, notebook filling, the idea settling. "In everything?" I asked, glancing at the passengers, their faces hinting at hidden depths. "Yes," he said, calm infinite. "See Brahma in one leaf, one thought, and you'll see it in all, flowing to its source."

"Start small," he said. "See Brahma in one moment." His calm made Brahma tangible, a truth woven into the infinite.

13: The Dance of Existence

The stranger's vision of Brahma as the infinite essence sparked a question. The Shivashahi bus rolled on, sugarcane fields under a sky heavy with clouds. "Why does Brahma become the world?" I asked, picturing the fields, the passengers, the chaos of Pune.

His smile was playful, his calm vast. "For joy," he said, voice clear. "Brahma dances, forms arise, play, dissolve—all for the delight of being, like a child building sandcastles, knowing they'll wash away." The words turned existence into a celebration.

I scribbled, heart racing. "Just for joy?" I asked, intrigued, picturing Pune's crowded streets, each scene vibrant. "Yes," he said, smile warm, his voice a gentle tide. "No reason, no goal—Brahma's joy is free, like the dawn, clear and eternal."

"How do I join the dance?" I asked, voice soft. "Live it," he said, detachment infinite. "See Brahma in every form, every moment, flowing to its source." I leaned back, notebook filling, the idea settling. "All part of the dance?" I asked, glancing at the passengers, their faces hinting at unique stories. "Yes," he said, calm infinite. "See the dance, know Brahma, like the dawn, clear and eternal."

14: The Hidden Self

The stranger's vision of Brahma's dance sparked a question. The Shivashahi bus rolled on, sugarcane fields under a sky heavy with clouds. "Where am I in Brahma's dance?" I asked, feeling both small and vast.

His gaze was serene, his calm vast. "You're not in it—you are it," he said, voice clear. "The 'you' you think you are—coder, son—is a mask. Brahma's the true self, hidden behind the mask, like the sky behind clouds." The words dissolved my sense of self, revealing a deeper truth.

I scribbled, heart pounding. "A mask?" I asked, picturing my Pune life—coding, stress, doubts. "Yes," he said, smile warm, his voice a gentle tide. "The mask feels real—your roles, fears, plans—but Brahma's the self, eternal, like the dawn, clear and eternal."

"How do I see the real self?" I asked, voice eager. "Look beyond the mask," he said, detachment infinite. "See what's aware, unchanging, flowing to its source." I leaned back, notebook filling, the idea settling. "The same self in them?" I asked, glancing at the passengers, their lives hinting at hidden depths. "One self, Brahma," he said, calm infinite. "See it in you, see it in all, like the dawn, clear and eternal."

35

15: Decoding the Mind

The stranger's revelation of Brahma as the true self sparked a question. The Shivashahi bus rolled on, sugarcane fields under a sky heavy with clouds. "If I'm Brahma, why don't I feel it?" I asked, picturing my restless thoughts.

His gaze was serene, his calm vast. "The mind hides it," he said, voice clear. "It spins stories—roles, fears, wants—veiling Brahma, like clouds hiding the sun." The words framed my mind as a barrier.

I scribbled, heart racing. "My mind?" I asked, picturing Pune's noise—deadlines, chatter. "Yes," he said, smile warm, his voice a gentle tide. "It's Brahma's play too, but it traps you in stories, hiding the dawn, clear and eternal."

"How do I see past the mind?" I asked, voice soft. "Watch it," he said, detachment infinite. "See thoughts arise, pass, like clouds. Brahma's the sky, flowing to its source." I leaned back, notebook filling, the idea settling. "Everyone's mind hides it?" I asked, glancing at the passengers, their faces hinting at hidden stillness. "Yes," he said, calm infinite. "Watch the mind, find Brahma, like the dawn, clear and eternal."

16: Guides or Illusions?

The stranger's vision of the mind as Brahma's play sparked a question. The Shivashahi bus rolled on, sugarcane fields under a sky heavy with clouds. "What about gurus, books—do I need them?" I asked, picturing my spiritual texts.

His gaze was serene, his calm vast. "They point, but aren't the truth," he said, voice clear. "Gurus, books—they're Brahma's play too, but the mind clings, making them illusions if you don't look beyond, like maps mistaken for the land." The words reframed my guides as tools, not truths.

I scribbled, heart racing. "No guides at all?" I asked, picturing my Pune searches, endless blogs. "Use them," he said, smile warm, his voice a gentle tide. "But test them, see for yourself, like the dawn, clear and eternal."

"How do I know what's true?" I asked, voice soft. "Feel it," he said, detachment infinite. "Truth resonates, like Brahma's silence, flowing to its source." I leaned back, notebook filling, the idea settling. "Everyone needs guides?" I asked, glancing at the passengers, their lives hinting at hidden quests. "At first," he said, calm infinite. "Then Brahma guides, like the dawn, clear and eternal."

17: Words Without Wings

The stranger's view of guides as pointers sparked a question. The Shivashahi bus rolled on, sugarcane fields under a sky heavy with clouds. "Can words ever hold Brahma?" I asked, picturing my notebook's pages.

His gaze was serene, his calm vast. "Words fly, but don't reach," he said, voice clear. "They're Brahma's play, pointing to the infinite, but Brahma's beyond, like the sky—words are birds, flying but never touching the sky itself." The words humbled my urge to define.

I scribbled, heart stirring. "No words at all?" I asked, picturing my Pune debates, endless explanations. "Use them," he said, smile warm, his voice a gentle tide. "But know their limit, like the dawn, clear and eternal."

"How do I share without words?" I asked, voice soft. "Live it," he said, detachment infinite. "Your life speaks, like Brahma's silence, flowing to its source." I leaned back, notebook filling, the idea settling. "Words always fail?" I asked, picturing my urge to write. "They point," he said, calm infinite. "But Brahma's felt, like the dawn, clear and eternal."

41

18: The Endless Why

The stranger's vision of words as pointers sparked a question. The Shivashahi bus rolled on, sugarcane fields under a sky heavy with clouds. "Why do I keep asking why?" I asked, picturing my endless questions.

His gaze was serene, his calm vast. "The 'why' is Brahma's pull," he said, voice clear. "It's the mind seeking its source, like a river flowing to the sea, endless until it merges." The words turned my questions into a sacred quest.

I scribbled, heart racing. "It never stops?" I asked, picturing Pune's sleepless nights, questions piling. "It stops in knowing," he said, smile warm, his voice a gentle tide. "When you see Brahma, the 'why' dissolves, like the dawn, clear and eternal."

"How do I stop asking?" I asked, voice soft. "See the asker," he said, detachment infinite. "The 'you' asking is Brahma, flowing to its source." I leaned back, notebook filling, the idea settling. "Everyone asks why?" I asked, glancing at the passengers, their faces hinting at shared quests. "Yes," he said, calm infinite. "It's Brahma's call, like the dawn, clear and eternal."

19: Breaking Free from Faith

The stranger's vision of the 'why' as Brahma's pull sparked a question. The Shivashahi bus rolled on, sugarcane fields under a sky heavy with clouds. "What about faith—do I need it?" I asked, picturing my mother's prayers.

His gaze was serene, his calm vast. "Faith can spark seeking," he said, voice clear. "But clinging to it blinds, like mist hiding the sun. Brahma's known, not believed, like the sky—you see it, not trust it's there." The words reframed faith as a step, not the goal.

I scribbled, heart racing. "No faith at all?" I asked, picturing my Pune doubts, clinging to rituals. "Start with faith," he said, smile warm, his voice a gentle tide. "Then see for yourself, like the dawn, clear and eternal."

"How do I know without faith?" I asked, voice soft. "Look directly," he said, detachment infinite. "Brahma's here, like the dawn, clear and eternal." I leaned back, notebook filling, the idea settling. "Everyone starts with faith?" I asked, glancing at the passengers, their lives hinting at shared beliefs. "Most do," he said, calm infinite. "Knowing frees, like the dawn, clear and eternal."

20: Empty Rituals

The stranger's call to know Brahma directly sparked a question. The Shivashahi bus rolled on, sugarcane fields under a sky heavy with clouds. "What about rituals—do they help?" I asked, picturing my temple visits.

His gaze was serene, his calm vast. "Rituals can focus the mind," he said, voice clear. "But they're empty if they're just acts, like shells without the pearl—Brahma's the pearl, not the shell." The words stripped my rituals of weight.

I scribbled, heart racing. "No rituals at all?" I asked, picturing my Pune attempts, clinging to mantras. "Use them if they help," he said, smile warm, his voice a gentle tide. "But don't stop there—see Brahma, like the dawn, clear and eternal."

"How do I see past rituals?" I asked, voice soft. "Feel what's real," he said, detachment infinite. "Rituals point, Brahma lives, flowing to its source." I leaned back, notebook filling, the idea settling. "Everyone does rituals?" I asked, glancing at the passengers, their lives hinting at shared acts. "Many do," he said, calm infinite. "Truth's beyond, like the dawn, clear and eternal."

21: Time for Truth

The stranger's view of rituals as pointers sparked a question. The Shivashahi bus rolled on, sugarcane fields under a sky heavy with clouds. "How long to find Brahma?" I asked, picturing my years of seeking.

His gaze was serene, his calm vast. "Time's Brahma's play too," he said, voice clear. "Truth's here, now—waiting, like the sky, always present." The words dissolved my rush.

I scribbled, heart racing. "No waiting at all?" I asked, picturing my Pune schedules, always rushing. "None," he said, smile warm, his voice a gentle tide. "The mind says 'later,' but Brahma's now, like the dawn, clear and eternal."

"How do I see it now?" I asked, voice soft. "Stop looking ahead," he said, detachment infinite. "Brahma's here, like the dawn, clear and eternal." I leaned back, notebook filling, the idea settling. "Everyone waits?" I asked, glancing at the passengers, their faces hinting at shared impatience. "Most do," he said, calm infinite. "Truth's now, like the dawn, clear and eternal."

22: Lifting the Fog

The stranger's call to see Brahma now sparked a question. The Shivashahi bus rolled on, sugarcane fields under a sky heavy with clouds. "Why's it so hard to see Brahma?" I asked, picturing my failed meditations.

His gaze was serene, his calm vast. "The mind's fog hides it," he said, voice clear. "Thoughts, wants, fears—they cloud Brahma, like mist over the hills." The words framed my struggle as a fog.

I scribbled, heart racing. "My fog?" I asked, picturing Pune's noise—stress, doubts. "Yes," he said, smile warm, his voice a gentle tide. "It's Brahma's play too, but it veils the truth, like clouds hiding the dawn, clear and eternal."

"How do I clear it?" I asked, voice soft. "Watch the fog," he said, detachment infinite. "See thoughts, let them pass—Brahma shines, flowing to its source." I leaned back, notebook filling, the idea settling. "Everyone's foggy?" I asked, glancing at the passengers, their faces hinting at hidden clarity. "Most are," he said, calm infinite. "Clarity's Brahma, like the dawn, clear and eternal."

23: The Weight of Desire

The stranger's call to clear the mind's fog sparked a question. The Shivashahi bus rolled on, sugarcane fields under a sky heavy with clouds. "What about desires—do I give them up?" I asked, picturing my career goals.

His gaze was serene, his calm vast. "Desires are Brahma's play," he said, voice clear. "But clinging to them binds you, like chains in a dream—Brahma's free." The words reframed my wants as illusions.

I scribbled, heart racing. "No desires at all?" I asked, picturing Pune's ambitions—promotions, success. "Live them, don't cling," he said, smile warm, his voice a gentle tide. "See them as Brahma's dance, like the dawn, clear and eternal."

"How do I stop clinging?" I asked, voice soft. "See their root," he said, detachment infinite. "Desires pass—Brahma stays, flowing to its source." I leaned back, notebook filling, the idea settling. "Everyone clings?" I asked, glancing at the passengers, their faces hinting at shared chains. "Most do," he said, calm infinite. "Freedom's Brahma, like the dawn, clear and eternal."

24: The Mirror of Awareness

The stranger's vision of desires as Brahma's play sparked a question. The Shivashahi bus rolled on, sugarcane fields under a sky heavy with clouds. "How do I stay aware to see Brahma?" I asked, picturing my distracted mind. His gaze was serene, his calm vast. "Awareness is Brahma's mirror," he said, voice clear. "It reflects truth—thoughts, desires, the world—all seen in awareness, which is Brahma itself." The words made awareness a gateway.

I scribbled, heart racing. "My awareness?" I asked, picturing Pune's distractions—notifications, noise. "Yes," he said, smile warm, his voice a gentle tide. "It's Brahma, always there, like the dawn, clear and eternal."

"How do I stay in it?" I asked, voice soft. "Rest in it," he said, detachment infinite. "Don't chase—be aware, like the dawn, clear and eternal." I leaned back, notebook filling, the idea settling. "Everyone can be aware?" I asked, glancing at the passengers, their faces hinting at hidden clarity. "Yes," he said, calm infinite. "Awareness is Brahma, flowing to its source."

25: The Illusion of Control

The stranger's call to rest in awareness sparked a question. The Shivashahi bus rolled on, sugarcane fields under a sky heavy with clouds. "What about control—do I let it go?" I asked, picturing my schedules.

His gaze was serene, his calm vast. "Control's an illusion," he said, voice clear. "Brahma flows, forms arise, dissolve—you're Brahma, not the controller, like the sky, not the storm." The words dissolved my grip.

I scribbled, heart racing. "No control at all?" I asked, picturing Pune's plans—deadlines, goals. "Act, don't grasp," he said, smile warm, his voice a gentle tide. "See Brahma's flow, like the dawn, clear and eternal."

"How do I let go?" I asked, voice soft. "See the controller," he said, detachment infinite. "It's a thought—Brahma flows, like the dawn, clear and eternal." I leaned back, notebook filling, the idea settling. "Everyone tries to control?" I asked, glancing at the passengers, their faces hinting at shared illusions. "Most do," he said, calm infinite. "Freedom's Brahma, flowing to its source."

Bus to Bliss: A Techie's Coincidental Journey With A Spiritual Master

26: The Roots of Suffering

The stranger's vision of control as an illusion sparked a question. The Shivashahi bus rolled on, sugarcane fields under a sky heavy with clouds. "Why do I suffer if I'm Brahma?" I asked, picturing my stress.

His gaze was serene, his calm vast. "Suffering's the mind's resistance," he said, voice clear. "You fight Brahma's flow—wanting, fearing, clinging—suffering grows, like weeds in a garden." The words rooted my pain in resistance.

I scribbled, heart racing. "My resistance?" I asked, picturing Pune's stress—deadlines, failures. "Yes," he said, smile warm, his voice a gentle tide. "It's Brahma's play too, but it veils joy, like clouds hiding the dawn, clear and eternal."

"How do I stop resisting?" I asked, voice soft. "See the resistance," he said, detachment infinite. "Let it be—Brahma flows, like the dawn, clear and eternal." I leaned back, notebook filling, the idea settling. "Everyone resists?" I asked, glancing at the passengers, their faces hinting at shared pain. "Most do," he said, calm infinite. "Joy's Brahma, flowing to its source."

27: The Joy Within

The stranger's vision of suffering as resistance sparked a question. The Shivashahi bus rolled on, sugarcane fields under a sky heavy with clouds. "Where's the joy Brahma promises?" I asked, picturing my rare moments of happiness.

His gaze was serene, his calm vast. "Joy's your essence," he said, voice clear. "It's Brahma, always there, uncovered when resistance fades, like the sun when clouds part." The words made joy my nature.

I scribbled, heart racing. "Always there?" I asked, picturing Pune's stress, joy buried. "Yes," he said, smile warm, his voice a gentle tide. "The mind covers it—rest in Brahma, like the dawn, clear and eternal."

"Just rest?" I asked, picturing my restless mind. "Yes," he said, detachment infinite. "No chasing, no fighting. Brahma's joy is you, like the dawn, clear and eternal." I leaned back, notebook filling, the idea settling. "In everyone?" I asked, glancing at the passengers, their lives hinting at hidden joys. "Always," he said, calm infinite. "Uncover it by seeing Brahma, flowing to its source."

28: Beyond Good and Evil

The stranger's vision of joy within led to a question rooted in my parents' teachings, where morality shaped my choices. The stranger's calm, a quiet force beside me, his white kurta catching sunlight, urged me to voice the confusion in my chest. "What about right and wrong?" I asked, picturing my father's lessons on duty.

His gaze was serene, his calm vast. "Good, evil—they're labels," he said. "Brahma's beyond, whole, embracing all. Enlightenment sees actions, not judgments, flowing from unity." The words reframed my values, urging clarity over division.

I scribbled, heart racing. "No morality at all?" I asked, unease creeping, picturing my father's teachings. "Act with care," he said, smile warm, his voice a gentle tide. "Labels are mind's play, like clouds passing without trace."

"How do I act without labels?" I asked, voice soft. "See all as Brahma," he said, detachment infinite. "Care flows, no 'good,' no 'evil,' like the dawn, clear and eternal." I leaned back, notebook filling, the idea settling. "Everyone judges?" I asked, glancing at the passengers, their lives hinting at shared judgments. "Yes," he said, calm infinite. "Freedom's beyond, like the dawn, clear and eternal."

29: The Eternal Now

The stranger's vision of acting beyond labels sparked a question rooted in my Pune schedules, where time drove my days. The stranger's calm, a quiet force beside me, his white kurta catching sunlight, urged me to voice the tension in my chest. "What about past and future?" I asked, picturing my plans.

His gaze was serene, his calm vast. "Time's a trick of the mind," he said, voice clear. "Brahma's the eternal now, beyond past or future, flowing without end." The words pulled me to the present, freeing time's grip.

I scribbled, heart racing. "No future at all?" I asked, picturing my Pune deadlines. "Live now," he said, smile warm, his voice a gentle tide. "Plans are Brahma's play, not truth, passing without trace."

"How do I stay in the now?" I asked, voice soft. "See this moment," he said, detachment infinite. "Brahma's here, like the dawn, clear and eternal." I leaned back, notebook filling, the idea settling. "Everyone trapped in time?" I asked, glancing at the passengers, their lives hinting at shared delays. "Yes," he said, calm infinite. "Freedom's now, flowing to its source."

30: The Infinite Within

The stranger's vision of the eternal now sparked a question. The stranger's calm, a quiet force beside me, his white kurta catching sunlight, urged me to voice the awe in my chest. "Is Brahma really in me?" I asked, voice soft.

He nodded, gaze serene, his calm vast. "You're Brahma," he said, voice clear. "Not a spark, the whole, infinite and joyful. Enlightenment's knowing this, flowing through all." The words made me limitless.

I scribbled, heart pounding. "Me? Infinite?" I asked, pen trembling, picturing my Pune life—coding, stress, doubts—small. "Yes," he said, smile warm, his voice a gentle tide. "Coder, son—these are roles. Brahma's your core, like the dawn, clear and eternal."

"How do I know it?" I asked, voice eager. "Rest in awareness," he said, detachment infinite. "See 'you' beyond roles. Brahma shines, flowing to its source." I leaned back, notebook filling, the idea settling. "In them too?" I asked, glancing at the passengers, their lives hinting at hidden infinities. "In all," he said, calm infinite. "Know it in you, see it everywhere, flowing to its source."

31: The Play of Forms

The stranger's revelation that I was Brahma, infinite within, sparked a question. The stranger's calm, a quiet force beside me, his white kurta catching sunlight, urged me to voice the wonder in my chest. "Why so many forms—people, things?" I asked, eyeing the passengers.

His smile was playful, his calm vast. "Brahma's joy," he said. "Like ocean waves, forms arise, dance, dissolve, each a play of Brahma's light." The words turned diversity into a cosmic dance.

I scribbled, heart racing. "For fun?" I asked, intrigued, picturing Pune's crowds, each unique. "Yes," he said, smile warm, his voice a gentle tide. "Brahma plays, no why, flowing without need."

"How do I see them as play?" I asked, voice soft. "Watch forms arise, pass," he said, detachment infinite. "See Brahma in each, flowing to its source." I leaned back, notebook filling, the idea settling. "All forms Brahma?" I asked, glancing at the passengers, their faces hinting at unique stories. "Yes," he said, calm infinite. "See the play, know the player, like the dawn, clear and eternal."

32: The Silence of Truth

The stranger's vision of forms as Brahma's play sparked a question. "How do I touch Brahma's truth?" I asked, craving its essence.

His gaze was serene, his calm vast. "Silence is its voice," he said, voice clear. "Beyond words, thoughts, Brahma speaks in stillness, eternal and quiet." The words painted truth as a silent presence. I scribbled, heart racing. "Silence?" I asked, picturing my Pune noise—deadlines, chatter. "Yes," he said, smile warm, his voice a gentle tide. "Rest in stillness, beyond mind's noise, like the dawn, clear and eternal."

"How do I find silence?" I asked, voice soft. "Watch the mind, let it settle," he said, detachment infinite. "Silence is Brahma, flowing to its source." I leaned back, notebook filling, the idea settling. "Everyone can find silence?" I asked, glancing at the passengers, their faces hinting at hidden stillness. "Yes," he said, calm infinite. "Rest in awareness, flowing to its source."

33: The Fire of Inquiry

The stranger's vision of silence as Brahma's voice ignited a question. The stranger's calm, a quiet force beside me, his white kurta catching sunlight, urged me to voice the urgency burning in my chest. "How do I keep seeking Brahma?" I asked.

His gaze was serene, eyes warm yet piercing, his calm vast. "Inquiry is the fire," he said, voice clear. "Question deeply, relentlessly, burning through illusions to Brahma." The words set my heart ablaze, transforming doubt into a sacred tool.

I scribbled, hand trembling. "Question everything?" I asked, voice eager, picturing my Pune debates, where logic clashed with faith. "Yes," he said, smile warm, his voice a gentle tide. "Doubt is Brahma's call, a flame that burns to truth, eternal in every moment."

"How do I question deeply?" I asked, voice soft. "Ask 'Who am I?'" he said, detachment infinite. "Burn with it, peel the layers—coder, son, dreamer—until Brahma shines, like the dawn, clear and eternal." I leaned back, notebook filling, the idea settling. "Can everyone inquire like this?" I asked, glancing at the passengers, their lives hinting at hidden quests. "Yes," he said, calm infinite. "Inquiry's universal, a fire in every heart, flowing to its source."

34: The Unity of All

The stranger's call to inquiry sparked a question. The stranger's calm, a quiet force beside me, his white kurta catching sunlight, urged me to voice the wonder stirring in my chest. "Is everything one, truly?" I asked, gazing at the passengers, their diverse faces a tapestry of lives.

His smile was radiant, his calm vast. "Yes," he said, voice clear. "Brahma's the one, infinite, whole, appearing as many—fields, people, stars—no separation, flowing through all, eternal in every moment." The words wove the universe into a single thread.

I scribbled, heart pounding. "No 'other' at all?" I asked, voice soft, picturing Pune's crowded streets, each face unique yet one. "None," he said, gaze warm, his voice a gentle tide. "The mind sees 'other,' but Brahma's the whole, embracing every ripple."

"How do I see this oneness?" I asked, voice eager. "Look beyond forms," he said, detachment infinite. "See Brahma in all—friend, stranger, pain, joy—like the dawn, clear and eternal." I leaned back, notebook filling, the idea settling. "In conflict too?" I asked, picturing Pune's arguments, my team's clashes. "Yes," he said, calm infinite. "Conflict's a wave, Brahma's the ocean, flowing to its source."

35: The Veil of Words

The stranger's vision of Brahma's unity sparked a question. "How do I share Brahma's truth?" I asked, imagining teaching others.

His gaze was serene, his calm vast. "Words are veils," he said, voice clear. "They point to Brahma, but aren't it, like maps, not the water itself. Live the truth, let your life speak." The words tempered my enthusiasm, urging embodiment over explanation.

I scribbled, heart stirring. "No teaching at all?" I asked, picturing my Pune friends, eager to share. "Teach by being," he said, smile warm, his voice a gentle tide. "Words spark, but life's the flame, flowing to its source."

"How do I live it?" I asked, voice soft. "Be Brahma," he said, detachment infinite. "Act with awareness, love, no veil, like the dawn, clear and eternal." I leaned back, notebook filling, the idea settling. "Can words help at all?" I asked, picturing my urge to write. "If lived," he said, calm infinite. "Speak from Brahma, not ego, flowing to its source."

36: The Weight of Doubt

The stranger's call to live Brahma's truth stirred a confession. The stranger's calm, a quiet force beside me, his white kurta catching sunlight, urged me to voice the fear in my chest. "What if I doubt all this?" I asked, voice low, shame creeping, picturing my wavering faith in Pune's sleepless nights.

His eyes softened, his calm vast. "Doubt's a gift," he said. "It's Brahma's whisper, urging clarity." The words turned my fear into a tool, easing my doubts about enlightenment.

I scribbled, heart lifting. "Embrace doubt?" I asked, pen racing, hope flickering, picturing my Pune struggles. "Yes," he said, smile warm, his voice a gentle tide. "Let doubt burn, question deeply, finding Brahma's truth, eternal in every moment."

"What if doubt overwhelms?" I asked, voice soft. "Let it," he said, detachment infinite. "Doubt leads to Brahma, flowing to its source." I leaned back, notebook filling, the idea settling. "Everyone doubts?" I asked, glancing at the passengers, their lives hinting at shared uncertainty. "Yes," he said, calm infinite. "Doubt's universal, a call to truth, flowing to its source."

37: The Dance of Detachment

The stranger's embrace of doubt as Brahma's call sparked a question. "How do I detach without losing what I love?" I asked, picturing my family, my career.

His gaze was serene, his calm vast. "Detachment's not loss," he said, voice clear. "It's Brahma's dance, loving without clinging, flowing freely, eternal in every moment." The words eased my fear, reframing love as light.

I scribbled, heart racing. "Love without holding?" I asked, picturing my parents, my Pune dreams. "Yes," he said, smile warm, his voice a gentle tide. "Hold lightly, see them as Brahma's play."

"How do I love like that?" I asked, voice soft. "See Brahma in them," he said, detachment infinite. "Love flows, no chains, like the dawn, clear and eternal." I leaned back, notebook filling, the idea settling. "Everyone clings?" I asked, glancing at the passengers, their lives hinting at shared attachments. "Yes," he said, calm infinite. "Freedom's loving without grip, flowing to its source."

38: The Light of Compassion

The stranger's vision of detachment as Brahma's dance sparked a question. "Does detachment mean I stop caring?" I asked, picturing my family's kindness.

His smile was radiant, his calm vast. "Detachment deepens care," he said, voice clear. "Compassion's Brahma's light, flowing from unity, not clinging, nurturing all without grasp." The words reframed kindness as boundless.

I scribbled, heart racing. "Care without clinging?" I asked, picturing my Pune struggles, helping colleagues yet seeking praise. "Yes," he said, smile warm, his voice a gentle tide. "See all as Brahma, care flows freely, like the dawn, clear and eternal."

"How do I care like that?" I asked, voice soft. "Act from unity," he said, detachment infinite. "No 'other' to save, only Brahma, flowing to its source." I leaned back, notebook filling, the idea settling. "Everyone can care this way?" I asked, glancing at the passengers, their lives hinting at hidden kindness. "Yes," he said, calm infinite. "Compassion's Brahma's nature, flowing to its source."

39: The End of Seeking

The stranger's vision of compassion as Brahma's light sparked a question. "When does seeking end?" I asked, craving completion.

His gaze was serene, his calm vast. "Seeking ends in knowing," he said, voice clear. "You're Brahma, whole, here, now. Enlightenment's resting in this, already home, eternal in every moment." The words dissolved my quest, revealing I was the goal.

I scribbled, heart pounding. "No more questions?" I asked, picturing my Pune searches, endless blogs. "Questions fade," he said, smile warm, his voice a gentle tide. "You're the answer, Brahma, like the dawn, clear and eternal."

"How do I rest?" I asked, voice soft. "See you're whole," he said, detachment infinite. "No lack, no chase, flowing to its source." I leaned back, notebook filling, the idea settling. "Everyone finds this?" I asked, glancing at the passengers, their lives hinting at hidden wholeness. "All can," he said, calm infinite. "Rest in Brahma, flowing to its source."

40: The Touch of Eternity

As Pune's skyline loomed, a faint haze of urban sprawl, the stranger's vision of seeking's end sparked a question. The Shivashahi bus wound through the landscape, sugarcane fields fading into patches of concrete. "Have I touched Brahma?" I asked, feeling a spark from our talk.

His gaze softened, his calm vast. "You've glimpsed it," he said, voice clear. "Your questions, your peace—they're Brahma's touch, like a sparkle under dawn's light, eternal in every moment." The words confirmed a shift within, my heart lighter.

I scribbled, heart racing. "Glimpses?" I asked, pen racing, picturing Pune's quiet evenings, coding smoothly, feeling alive. "Yes," he said, smile warm, his voice a gentle tide. "Each question, each calm, is Brahma's touch, like the dawn, clear and eternal."

"How do I hold it?" I asked, voice soft. "Live it," he said, detachment infinite. "See Brahma in every moment, flowing to its source." I leaned back, notebook filling, the idea settling. "In everyone's moments?" I asked, glancing at the passengers, their lives hinting at hidden glimpses. "Yes," he said, calm infinite. "Live the glimpse, know Brahma, flowing to its source."

41: A Journey Unfinished

The Shivashahi bus rolled into Pune's chaotic bus stand, a swirl of horns, hawkers, and diesel fumes, pulling me from the infinite to the ordinary. It was June 7, 2021, just past 11:30 AM, and the two-and-a-half-hour ride had reshaped my soul. The stranger stood, his white kurta pristine, his calm radiating oneness with the infinite, untouched by the bustle. His eyes, warm yet piercing, met mine, a final beacon in the urban sprawl. "Keep seeking Brahma," he said, voice soft, slicing through the noise.

As he stepped into the aisle, a phone rang in his pocket, a rare intrusion into his serene presence. He answered, voice low, and I caught a name—"Indrajit"—spoken by the caller, a fleeting revelation that anchored the mysterious stranger in a name, Indrajit Bagal, yet left his essence boundless. Before I could speak, ask for more, he slipped into the crowd, a silhouette dissolving into Pune's pulse, now a tech hub where the river wound through centuries of stories. I stood frozen, bag heavy, notebook brimming with his truths—Brahma's unity, the dream of life, the joy within.

Pune's bus stand buzzed, a microcosm of the urban heart. I lingered, Indrajit's words anchoring me, his calm a mirror to the timeless spirit. Who was he? A sage, Brahma itself in human form, his teachings flowing boundless? Back in my Kharadi flat, I pored over my notebook, his insights guiding my meditation, softening my doubts, lightening my coder's life of deadlines and stress. I searched for him, but he was a shadow, gone, yet his truth took root, urging me to see Brahma in every moment.

Now, in May 2025, I write from New York, where I've lived since December 2022, working in IT amid Manhattan's skyscrapers, their gleam a far cry from India's landscapes. The journey that began on that bus has grown, weaving through years of change, discovery, and deeper truths. To avoid lengthening this book, I'll save the fuller story for a sequel.

The sequel will recount how I found Indrajit Bagal again, tracking him through Pune's spiritual circles to his modest home, where his calm, one with Brahma, remained a beacon. It will detail our annual meetings in India, each visit a lantern on my path, his words sharpening my practice. I'll describe my move to the USA, leaving Pune's urban sprawl for New York's neon pulse, coding by day, seeking Brahma by night, guided by Indrajit's wisdom. I'll share how I urged him to write Infinite Bliss, published after tireless effort, its translations in German, Spanish, and French carrying his truth worldwide. It will paint Indrajit's routine—dawn meditations, teaching disciples, evening walks by the river, his steps light, his family sharing simple joys, his low-profile life a silent sermon, eternal and unassuming.

For now, seekers, read Infinite Bliss: The Simplest Way to Enlightenment to delve deeper into Brahma's truth, written by Indrajit Bagal. My journey's unfinished, a path winding through New York's streets, each step lit by a mysterious stranger whose calm, one with Brahma, flows boundless yet grounded.

Printed in Dunstable, United Kingdom